THE GIRL WHO FELL FROM THE SKY

and Other Classic Philippine Legends

A TREASURY OF PHILIPPINE FOLK TALES

THE GIRL WHO FELL
FROM THE SKY

and Other Classic Philippine Legends

as told by MARIA ELENA PATERNO

Illustrated by ALBERT GAMOS

Tahanan Books for Young Readers
M A N I L A

Published in the Philippines 1993 by Tahanan Books for Young Readers
A division of Tahanan Pacific, Inc.
P.O. Box 9079 | MCS Mailing Center
1299 Makati, Metro Manila
Philippines

Exclusively distributed in the United States by PaperWorks
P.O. Box 2851, Kirkland, WA 98083-2851

Cover design by Roberto T. Canlas
Book design and vignettes by Beth Parrocha
Printed in the Philippines by Island Graphics
First Hardcover Edition
2 4 6 8 10 9 7 5 3 1

ISBN 971-630-025-5 (pbd.)

This book is printed on recycled paper manufactured in the Philippines.

Contents

Introduction ❖ 7

The Girl Who Fell from the Sky
The Legend of Bohol Island ❖ 9

The Greedy Neighbor
The Legend of Lake Danum ❖ 14

Lord Laon and the Seven-Headed Dragon
The Legend of Mount Kanlaon ❖ 20

The Spring of Tears
The Legend of Salinas Spring ❖ 28

The Hunter's Promise
The Legend of Magat River ❖ 33

Battle Island
The Legend of Apo Island ❖ 39

The Queen Whom Love Forgot
The Legend of Mount Malindig ❖ 44

The Folly of the Seven Sisters
The Legend of Siete Pecadas ❖ 50

Sources of the Stories ❖ 55

For Further Reading ❖ 55

Introduction

Retold in this book are myths and legends gleaned from different parts of the Philippines. Although their origins are forgotten, the stories have survived. Countless generations of storytellers—and the listeners who made the stories their own—have fashioned and refashioned these tales until they became mirrors of their lives.

Most of the legends in this collection seek to explain the world in which we live: Why does Magat River run through the town? Why is Apo Island dangerous? Why is the Salinas Spring salty?

The answers our ancestors sought were not grounded in science. They emanated from two very basic questions: *Who are we?* And *why are we here?*

Scholars tell us that myths perform a number of functions. A myth is a journey inward, to unlock the mysteries of ourselves and the universe. Myths provide an explanation for what has shaped our natural world, but always in the face of a deep unfathomable mystery. The late author, Joseph Campbell, described mythology as "a song of the imagination." Through myths, he said, we seek the "experience of being alive."

A myth also attempts to instruct. It uses symbols to help shape the individual to the group or society. Through its moral, it can impart a law or code of behavior. The myth can also be perceived as a group dream, wherein archetypal urges are manifested and dealt with.

And so in answer to the question "Why does Magat River run through the town?," we reply, not with a discussion of river sources and the force of the water carving a path through the land, but with the story of a crocodile who turns into a beautiful maiden, and a promise extracted from a hunter which is subsequently broken. The hunter is punished for his broken promise through eternity.

Rather than talk about geology and the formation of islands, legend explains the origin of Apo Island with a story of a battle lost and a brave leader who continues to watch over his people. The Apo metamorphosed into an island whose deadly shores protect the village from intruders.

In the legend of Salinas Spring, the tears of a faithful wife are transformed into a spring.

Beyond the numerous functions of myth, however, is the power such tales derive from their ancient origins. Think of the legends in this book as ancient threads that join our modern selves to others from the past. For despite new technology, the changing face of society, and the thousands of years between us and the origin of the legend, the human condition remains unchanged. The stories speak with the same resonance today as they did thousands of years ago.

The stories may have been altered slightly in my version, just as they have been changed in generations of retelling. I may have taken liberties in order to fill in gaps I thought needed filling, or added details where I thought the embellishment would help the story. Please do the same when you tell the story to the next person. Read them, make them your own, and pass them on. They are all *our* stories—the collective oral heritage of the Filipino people.

Maria Elena Paterno

The Girl Who Fell from the Sky
The Legend of Bohol Island

In the beginning there was no land for people to live on. There was just the world of the sky, with its soft cool clouds, and beneath it a vast lake. One day the daughter of the chief of the sky became ill. Her name was Mayang. Her body burned with a fever so hot that she seemed to be on fire. She would not eat. Each day she got weaker and weaker. Finally her worried father called the medicine man.

The medicine man examined the girl. He felt her forehead. He held her pale cold hand. And then he shook his head and said, "The only cure for her lies in the roots of the wild balete tree. You must dig around this tree and let her touch its roots. Only then will she get well."

So the chief ordered his servants to dig a hole around the tree. The balete was an old giant of a tree and its roots reached deep down under the clouds. When the hole was dug, the chief's servants made a harness and carefully lowered Mayang into the hole.

But Mayang had grown so thin that she slipped right through the harness! The poor girl fell. Down, down she went, faster and faster into the vast lake. She was too surprised to make a sound.

A group of wild ducks swimming in the lake saw the girl falling from high up in the sky. "Quick!" the biggest duck called to the other ducks. "We must catch her!"

Just in time five ducks swimming closely together formed a pillow of fluffy feathers. Mayang landed lightly on their backs.

When Mayang looked around, she saw nothing but water. Scared and feeling all alone, she began to cry.

Pagong the turtle happened to be swimming by and saw the girl crying. She was a kind old turtle who did not like to see anyone unhappy. "Don't cry, you poor thing," Pagong said. "What's the matter? Are the ducks bothering you?"

"Certainly, certainly not!" the ducks quacked. "We saved her and are keeping her afloat on our backs!"

"Yes," said Mayang, who had recovered a little bit from her scare. "This is quite nice. These soft feathers remind me of the clouds of my home." But when she remembered her home she began to cry again.

Pagong eyed her curiously. She had never seen a little girl before. "What is your name, my dear?" she asked. "And where do you come from?"

"My name is Mayang and I come from...from up there." She pointed to the hole in the sky.

"I will help you," promised Pagong. "I just have to figure out a way."

And so Pagong called the animals of the lake to a meeting.

"We must help this poor girl," the big turtle told the animals.

"What's the matter with her?" asked Karpa, the lazy old fish. "Can't she swim?"

"No, I don't believe she can," answered Pagong. "Look how small her flippers are."

Suddenly Pagong had a bright idea.

"I have it," she cried. "What we must do is make a piece of land for her—an island!"

"M-m-make an island?" asked Alimasag the crab. "H-h-how?"

"Simple," said Pagong. She turned to Palaka, the young frog who was perched on a lily pad. "Your legs are long and your hind strokes can get you far." Palaka looked pleased. He was proud of his strong legs. "So," Pagong continued, "you must go down to the bottom of the lake and get some soil."

Palaka was only too pleased to show off. He disappeared, but before you could count to ten his head popped up again in the water. "It's too dark and spooky down there," he gasped. "Someone else must get the soil." With that Palaka paddled away.

"C-c-can I t-try?" asked Alimasag. "I am n-not a-afraid of the d-dark."

Alimasag disappeared into the water but soon she came up, sputtering. "Aaa-I c-could not find the bottom," she said. "So far it was!" And then she too swam away.

Now the ducks really began to complain. Pagong did not know

what to do. Suddenly she heard a low, throaty voice that said, "I'll "go-o-o." It came from an old toad.

The ducks complained even louder. Mayang was very heavy to carry. "Stop dreaming, old toad! If the frog couldn't do it, what makes you think you can? Too dangerous!" they quacked all at the same time.

But the toad had already dived into the darkness of the deep. The minutes passed. A long while later, the toad came up again. "I hob soil im my mouf," he said in his low voice.

"That's all right," said Pagong. "Thank you for—" Then she realized what the toad was saying. "You have it? The soil from the bottom of the lake is inside your mouth?"

Instead of answering, the toad opened his mouth. He spit the soil on the turtle's back and all the animals helped spread it around, until it became big enough for the girl.

Out of this soil an island grew, a big island, shaped like a turtle. The girl who had fallen from the sky lived on her new island. The island was called Bohol, and Mayang, the daughter of the sky chief, became the first Boholano.

The Greedy Neighbor
The Legend of Lake Danum

O nce upon a time, high up in the Cordillera mountains, there lived a young widow named Bulan. She was an honest, kind, and hard-working woman who tilled the fields her husband had left her and cared for her children as well as she could. But the weather had been bad that year. Too much rain had flooded the fields and killed the rice crop, so Bulan had nothing to feed her children.

One day while she was in the granary gathering up the last few grains of rice, Bulan heard her family's pig squeal under the house. It gave her an idea.

"I will take that pig to the market and trade it for rice," she said to her children. "Then at least we will have food to eat."

So the next day Bulan tied the pig in a basket, placed the basket on her head, and started on her journey. It was a warm day, and she tired easily because she was so hungry.

After a while she stopped to rest near a shallow lake. As she lifted the basket off her head the pig squealed out loud. All of a sudden, an old woman appeared. Her white hair seem to trap the sunlight and hold it. Her face was very pale, but her eyes were bright and clear.

"Where are you taking your pig?" the old woman asked. The old woman made her nervous, but Bulan answered truthfully and said, "I am going to Sagada to trade it for something to eat."

"Follow me. I will give you something for your pig," said the old woman. She walked to the edge of the lake and put out a foot. As Bulan watched in amazement, the old woman stepped onto the water. But her feet stayed dry. She walked a few steps on the shimmering silver surface of the lake and then turned to Bulan who still stood at the water's edge. Bulan shook her head uncertainly. She knew this was magic and she was frightened.

The old woman walked back to Bulan and held out her wrinkled hand. Balancing the basket on her head, Bulan took the old woman's hand. Slowly she stepped onto the lake. She waited to feel the wetness, but her feet never went under. It was like walking on a bed of soft moss.

Suddenly a small house on stilts appeared in the middle of the lake. The two women went inside, and Bulan set the basket with the pig down on the floor. The old woman sat on a stool by the window and ordered Bulan to pick the lice from her head. Bulan was more scared than ever, because now she was sure that the old woman was a witch. Yet Bulan did as she was told.

When Bulan parted the old woman's hair, she found no lice, only small snakes and centipedes. There must have been thousands of them! Bulan bit her lip so she would not scream and bravely crushed the snakes and centipedes between her thumbnails.

After an hour the old woman told her to stop. She got up and collected the snakes and centipedes. She threw them in a pot of vegetable stew and began to cook them. After a while the witch indicated the food was ready and served them on plates made of human skulls. It was disgusting, but Bulan was prepared to eat this foul meal so that her children would not starve. Once again she bit her lip and pretended that nothing was unusual.

When they finished eating, the old woman gave Bulan two gabi roots and one rice stalk. "Go home now," the old woman said. "As soon as you reach your house, put the rice stalk in the granary. Boil the gabi." She did not say any more, not even goodbye.

Bulan was disappointed that all she got for her pig and her trouble were two gabi roots and one rice stalk. Nonetheless she thanked the old woman and went home. She put the rice stalk in the granary and boiled the gabi, just as the old woman had instructed.

When the gabi was cooked, Bulan took a knife to cut it up. And then she noticed something strange. No matter how much she sliced, the gabi stayed the same size! Soon she had a hundred slices of gabi on the table, more than enough for her children to eat. She knew then that this was the old woman's gift.

Then she remembered the rice stalk and she ran to her granary. It was overflowing with rice! Bulan was very happy, because she knew that her family would never be hungry again.

Soon the neighbors began to notice Bulan's good fortune. One of her neighbors was a rich but greedy woman named Galay. This woman had refused to lend Bulan any rice when she had nothing to feed her children. Galay now asked Bulan how she came to have so much food. Bulan truthfully told Galay all about her strange journey.

"I will take my husband's pig and look for the old witch," said Galay with a hard glitter in her eyes.

"But your granary is full!" exclaimed Bulan.

"Ah, but if I had the magic rice stalk I would never have to work again!" said Galay, as she walked away to check on the pig.

The next day the greedy neighbor set out for the lake with a pig in a basket on her head. When she reached the lake she set her pig down. She pinched its tail to make sure it would squeal.

In a twinkling, the old woman appeared. Everything happened exactly as Bulan had told her.

The two women walked on the surface of the lake until they reached the house on stilts. The old woman took a stool, sat by the window, and told Galay to pick her lice. Galay was horrified and refused. Next the old woman made supper. But when Galay saw the plates made of human skulls she quickly got up from the table. As Galay ran toward the door, the old woman slapped her on the thigh. Instantly Galay turned into a big pine tree. The house and the old woman vanished. Only the lake and the tree remained.

A few years later a woodcutter came and saw the huge pine tree standing in the middle of the shallow lake. He decided to cut it down.

As soon as the tree fell, the water began to rise. The lake swallowed up much of the surrounding land and became so deep you could not see the bottom.

Today it is called Lake Danum, which means *lake water*. The pine tree no longer stands, but people believe that the greedy neighbor's spirit still lives in the middle of the lake.

Lord Laon and the Seven-Headed Dragon
The Legend of Mount Kanlaon

Once upon a time in a kingdom on the island of Negros, there lived a beautiful princess named Anina. Her eyes were soft black like the night and her lips were red. Her skin was clear and smooth. Princess Anina was destined to be queen after her father's death. And all the people loved her.

It was a happy kingdom, but now that the time of the cool winds was approaching, a terrible silence came over the land. The priestesses, who served as the king's advisers, were worried about something terribly important. Princess Anina, who led a very sheltered life, did not know what it was. The priestesses left the temple early in the morning and returned only at dusk. This they did, day after day, and it was clear that they could not find what they were looking for.

Finally the chief priestess came to the palace to report to the king. The princess was sitting beside her father as she spoke.

"We have searched all over the land, your highness," began the chief priestess. "The maidens are all marked. Not one of them will be acceptable to the dragon." She glanced at the princess. "Unless we find an unmarked young woman to sacrifice, we must prepare for the destruction and famine to come."

The princess was puzzled. What did the priestess mean? She looked to her father, but he was already dismissing the visitor with a wave of his hand. When they were alone Princess Anina's father gave a great sigh, and at long last spoke.

"It is time that you know. It happened in the reign of my father, your grandfather. The first of the attacks. We have an enemy, my daughter." He walked to the window and pointed outside.

"See that mountain? It is the highest in all of Negros. It is the home of a dragon. A frightful dragon, so long that its body coils three times around the mountain. It has seven heads, and each of its fourteen eyes glow like red hot coals. Its seven mouths belch blue and green fire, and all fourteen of its nostrils snort hot smoke and steam."

Princess Anina's blood ran cold. Why hadn't she been told this before? She saw how scared her father was. His eyes looked dull and hopeless as he told her how the dragon comes down from his mountain every five years. How the people see, first a glow on the mountain, and then a huge fire followed by white, hissing steam. All the bravest warriors had perished trying to fight the dragon. Anyone who came near had his skin scalded off and his sword melted from the dragon's heat.

The people found a way to appease the dragon only by accident. One day a young man and a young woman wandered close to the top of the mountain. Suddenly they felt a wind that smelled of rotten eggs. And then it happened so fast—a blue tongue, forked like a snake's but twenty times bigger, flicked down and lifted the girl up. The man ran all the way down the mountain for help. But they never saw the girl again.

"The next five years were years of peace and prosperity," continued the king. "And when the people saw once again the glow from the mountain they became very scared. They knew what would happen. It was the chief priestess who prepared the sacrifice."

But Princess Anina was shaking her head impatiently. Surely there was a better way to fight the dragon, she thought. But her father seemed to know what she was thinking and he gestured with his hand to make her listen.

"We do not know exactly what the dragon does with the maidens. But there is always a pool of blood. We have tried many things, but the dragon knows. The maiden offered for sacrifice must be young and unmarked. Otherwise the fires will come down, and there will be famine and destruction.

"It is a sacrifice," said the king, bowing his head. "But better one life than the entire kingdom's. There is no other way to fight this terrible dragon. I myself have tried, and I just barely escaped."

There was a long silence. Finally the princess spoke: "And that is why all the girls have marks on their faces. Now I understand, father."

The king embraced his daughter. "Forgive me. Your mother could not mar your face. When I insisted, she left the kingdom. So it fell on me to make the mark. But I could not. I had a knife ready. But I watched you sleeping, and I could not. Forgive me."

And then he let go of his daughter and stood tall before her. In a louder voice he said, "You will go from here. This afternoon you will set sail."

But the princess, who loved her people more than herself, said, "No, I will be the sacrifice. You know, father, that there is no one else. Better one life than the entire kingdom's. You said so yourself, my king."

The king bowed his head.

And so it was announced. The entire kingdom went into mourning. The priestesses made ready the black robes and the sleeping draught. The king sat on his throne with a face of stone. No one could talk to him, not even his daughter. Neither of them could say goodbye forever.

On the day the princess was to be taken to the dragon's mountain, a tall stranger appeared in the palace. The people could tell from his rich robes that he had come from the faraway land of India. The stranger stood before the king and said, "I have come to help."

But the king only said, "There is nothing any human can do against the dragon. But go, if you want. And if you succeed I shall reward you with all the riches in my kingdom."

The stranger bowed and left without another word. The king watched him go with sad eyes.

What the king did not know was that the stranger was really the great Khan Laon, or Lord Laon. He was strong and wise, and he had powers far greater than the sword that dangled by his side. Khan Laon could talk to all the beasts in their own language.

As he strode over to the slopes of the great mountain, Lord Laon spied an army of ants crawling on the ground. He saw bees flying around the bushes and eagles soaring in the great sky.

He bent on one knee and spoke to an ant: "I am your Lord Laon. Go quickly to your king. Tell him to gather his warriors and march to the top of the mountain. He must help me fight the dragon."

"Yes, Kahn Laon," replied the ant. It ran off.

Then Lord Laon got up and held out a finger. A bee came to rest on it. He spoke to the bee, saying: "I am your Lord Laon. Go quickly to your queen and tell her my command. She must send her bravest general to lead all the bees to the top of the mountain. She must help me fight the dragon."

"Yes, Khan Laon," replied the bee. It buzzed once and flew away.

Next Lord Laon lifted his sword and made a circle in the air. The eagles understood the sign and sent one of their own to perch on a tree branch. "Yes, my Lord?" asked the eagle.

"Fly to your king. Tell him my command. He must bring all the eagles to the top of the mountain. He must help me fight the dragon."

"Yes, Khan Laon." And the eagle lifted its great wings and soared into the sky.

The ants, the bees, and the eagles all did as Lord Laon commanded. The king of the eagles himself carried the brave Laon on his wings to the top of the mountain.

From the air they saw the dragon's green-gold body coiled around

the rocks. Suddenly, as if it had smelled something unusual, the dragon awoke. It lifted its seven heads and opened all fourteen of its terrible eyes. The dragon's nostrils snorted hot smoke. Its seven mouths blew out green and blue flames.

The sight of the flames in the distance sent a chill of fear throughout the valley. "The dragon is awake!" the people shouted. "The stranger will be killed!" The king sat numbly on his throne. The princess sat beside him, and her heart was beating fast. She was thinking about the brave man in the strange robes. She prayed for his safety.

The eagle set Lord Laon down on a spot burned black by the dragon's fire. There was an odor of rotten eggs. The dragon had not seen him yet, for it was still looking up at the sky. Lord Laon saw his chance. He signaled the attack.

In a flash, armies of ants began to swarm over the dragon's body. They crept under its great jagged scales and bit the soft, unprotected flesh. Then a swarm of bees flew in and stung all fourteen of the dragon's glowing red eyes until it was completely blind. Then the eagles swooped in and pecked the eyes out. Streams of black blood gushed out of the dragon's eye sockets.

The great beast was writhing in pain and slashing the air with its razor-sharp claws. Seven great mouths began spewing red flames into the sky. At last Lord Laon drew his sword and climbed the monster's terrible body. He chopped off its heads one by one. Blood spurted out from the dragon's necks, foul black blood, but when all of its heads were cut off, the terrible beast grew still. Its fires were silenced forever.

With a bow the great Lord Laon thanked the animals that helped him. Then he marched down the mountain. The people, who had been watching the fires on the top of the mountain, watched the glow die. "The dragon is dead!" they shouted.

Most of the villagers went to meet Khan Laon with great rejoicing. They gave him food and drink and water to clean himself. The princess thanked him. He took her hand and said, "I would like to serve you and your father, the king."

Lord Laon remained in the kingdom, and the king and Princess Anina learned to turn to him for advice. He was noble and wise, and soon he and the princess were married.

For this great adventure the people named the dragon's mountain Khan Laon. Today Mount Kanlaon still rises majestically over Negros Island, in memory of the great Lord Laon, who slew the seven-headed dragon.

The Spring of Tears

The Legend of Salinas Spring

Once upon a time in a village in the province of Nueva Vizcaya in the island of Luzon, there lived a beautiful maiden named Yumina. Yumina was as kind as she was beautiful, and many men wanted to marry her.

Yumina's father was a powerful chief, and he wanted a suitable husband for his daughter. But how to choose? Most of Yumina's suitors were rich and handsome. All of them said that they loved her.

The chief decided to hold a shooting contest. Yumina would stand against a tree with a bamboo tube under her right arm. Each man would have three chances to shoot an arrow through the tube. Whoever could shoot three arrows into the tube would get to marry Yumina. But whoever hit her instead would be put to death.

Many men prepared to join the contest. One of them was a handsome young man named Gumined.

Gumined and Yumina had been playmates when they were children and he wanted with all his heart to have Yumina for his wife. But he was not a rich man, so Gumined dared not propose marriage. When the contest was announced he saw his chance to win Yumina.

Gumined practiced shooting his arrows until his arms ached. "This is for Yumina," he told himself, "for I love her truly."

Another young man named Indawat also got ready for the contest. "My father is a good friend of Yumina's father," he told his friends. "I will surely win. Then our lands will be joined and we will be even more powerful." The boastful Indawat was so sure he would win that he never once touched his bow to practice.

On the day of the contest a big crowd came to watch. The suitors formed a line in the middle of a large field and waited. Ten of the oldest people in the village sat on one side of the field. They were the judges.

When Yumina came out, a sigh ran through the crowd. She was so beautiful! She walked with her head held high. Yumina calmly took her position by a tall *mabolo* tree, twenty paces in front of the contestants. She held the bamboo tube steadily under her arm. And she waited.

The contest began. One after the other, the men stepped up to the line and fired their arrows. Some succeeded in putting an arrow through the tube once, some even twice, but none could do it three times. Fortunately no arrow struck Yumina.

Then came Indawat's turn. He smiled confidently, but his first arrow almost hit the girl's side. Indawat angrily threw his bow to the

ground when he was asked to step aside.

Finally it was Gumined's turn. He looked at Yumina and saw her smiling. The smile encouraged him. Carefully he raised his bow and took aim. The arrow sailed through the air and flew straight into the bamboo tube under Yumina's arm.

The crowd gasped and then waited in silence. When Gumined's second arrow landed in the bamboo tube, some people actually clapped. The young man drew his bow for the third time, willing his beating heart to keep still. When the third arrow went through the tube, a wide smile spread across Yumina's face and her eyes lit up with joy. She raised her arms to welcome Gumined, who rushed up to her. "Your smile made my aim steady and sure," he said. Yumina embraced him. "I knew you would do it," she whispered.

They were married and lived happily together.

But still Indawat wanted Yumina for his wife. So he made a plan. He invited Gumined to a hunting party. Indawat ordered his men to lead Gumined to the deepest part of the forest and leave him there.

Indawat found Gumined in the forest. They were alone.

"Gumined, my friend," he raised his bow in greeting. "Let us share this hunt. A wild boar has just been through here. Look, its tracks lead to the cliffs. Quick, we must not let it escape."

The unsuspecting Gumined followed Indawat to the cliffs. When Gumined was near the cliff's edge, Indawat sprang forward and pushed him over. Gumined fell more than a thousand feet and was crushed on the rocks below. Then Indawat rolled a few big rocks off the cliff to make it look like Gumined was killed in a landslide.

Yumina's heart was heavy with grief. She buried Gumined in the field where the contest was held. Every morning she brought flowers to his grave, and every evening she lit a candle for him. She would not leave her husband's grave. "Bathala," she prayed. "Let me join my beloved. I cannot live without him."

One night the sky darkened. Lightning flashed and thunder rumbled over the land. Soon the rain fell in heavy sheets, until a great river of water roared through the field.

When the rain stopped, villagers found the lifeless body of Yumina still clinging to the grave of her beloved Gumined. When her father tried to remove her body, the earth shook and opened up. Yumina's body fell into a deep chasm. Then the earth closed again.

The next day the villagers were surprised to see a spring on the same spot where Yumina's body had disappeared. They tasted the water, but it was salty.

To this day the spring of Salinas is salty. The villagers say it is because Yumina still weeps for her beloved. And the waters are her tears.

The Hunter's Promise

The Legend of Magat River

A long time ago, in a town called Bayombong, in Nueva Vizcaya province, there lived a hunter named Magat. He was young and strong, his eyes were keen, and his hands sure and steady. He was swift as a deer and strong as a bull. Magat was the best hunter in the village, and proud of it.

He lived by himself in a small hut at the edge of the town. But he was a hunter who liked to spend most of his time outdoors. He did not like to be kept in, not by a house, nor by anyone's rules. And he was stubborn.

One day Magat was hunting in the forest. His sharp eyes spotted the tracks of a strange animal. They led to a part of the forest he had never explored, where it was cool and dark. Magat was curious, so he followed the tracks. The soil beneath his feet soon became mossy and full of soft, fallen leaves. Suddenly the tracks disappeared. Magat had to squint to see where he was. The trees were so tall that their branches interlocked overhead. There was hardly any sunlight in this part of the forest.

Then he heard the sound of running water.

Just beyond a clump of grass Magat saw a large stream. On the other side of the stream he saw a large balete tree with branches that leaned over the water. And there in the shade of the tree was a maiden, bathing.

Magat hid himself behind the tall grass. He sat very still and silent.

The mysterious woman bathed in slow graceful movements. She was the most beautiful woman Magat had ever seen. She had long black hair and her long arms skimmed through the water. Magat felt his heart stir in his chest. He could not take his eyes off her.

Just then his keen eyes detected a sudden movement. It seemed to come from the tree branch hanging just above the woman. Although it was hard to tell in the forest dark, his hunter's instinct told him that danger was near.

Just then a shaft of sunlight streamed through the leaves. The light revealed a python! The huge snake was coiled around the branch, ready to attack the woman.

In one swift movement Magat took his spear and aimed. Hearing a noise in the grass, the young woman looked up to see the hunter for the first time. He was tall and brown and strong, with a spear aimed right at her. She ducked under water at the same time that the python sprang.

The spear flew and hit its target. The huge snake fell writhing into the water.

Magat ran splashing across the stream. "Are you hurt?" he called out to the maiden.

The confused woman scrambled quickly onto the riverbank, but when she saw the dead python she stopped. Slowly she turned to stare at Magat. She now understood what had happened and hid her face in her hands. She was ashamed to have suspected him of wanting to hurt her, when really he had saved her life.

Magat took her hands gently and said, "Do not be afraid. I am only a poor hunter."

The maiden looked up at him and smiled. Magat felt his heart overflow with tenderness. They spent the rest of the day together, wandering in the cool forest. By the time the crickets began to sing and the moon had risen in the sky, the hunter had asked the lovely maiden to become his wife.

She agreed.

"I must ask of you only one thing," she said, taking his strong brown hand and putting it to her cheek. "You must promise, in the name of the great god Kabunian, never to look in on me at midday. If you swear it, I will become your wife."

"I will promise you anything," said Magat. "Just be my wife."

"Swear it," she said, urgently.

Magat thought to himself, "I am a hunter. I am always gone at midday. This will be an easy promise to keep." And so he swore never to lay eyes on her in the middle of the day. Then he laughed and said,

"Come, do not be so serious. We will be happy together."

And so they were. She made his home warm and cozy. She filled it with her lovely songs and the good smell of cooking.

One morning Magat was hunting in the forest, following the trail of a huge wild boar. He would have caught it too, but its hide was so tough that the shaft of his spear broke. "What use is a hunter without his spear?" he thought to himself. Not realizing that it was midday, he decided to head for home.

When he arrived at his hut, everything was quiet. It seemed that no one was home. Then Magat saw that the door to his bedroom was closed. Suddenly he remembered his promise to his wife. He took another spear and left in a hurry so that he wouldn't be tempted to look.

But Magat became curious. He found himself going home at noon the next day, and again the day after. "It is my home after all and she is my wife," he reasoned. "Married people should have no secrets."

And so one midday Magat came home and quietly opened the bedroom door a crack and peeked in. To his horror, he saw a great crocodile lying on his wife's bed. Quickly he ran out to get his spear. Then he crashed into the bedroom, spear poised to strike, but he stopped short.

Lying on his bed was his wife. She appeared sick and pale. When he drew near, she whispered, "You broke your promise, and now I must die. I can no longer live on this earth as your wife. I must leave you."

And as Magat watched in horror, her skin changed color and grew thick. Her arms and legs shortened and her hands and feet became claws. Slimy green scales began to form on her smooth skin. Before his very eyes she had turned into a crocodile. He had broken a promise made in the name of the god Kabunian.

Magat carried the dead crocodile outside and buried it in his yard. He blamed himself for his wife's death and could not bear to eat or sleep. At last, worn out by sorrow and grief, Magat drowned himself in the very stream where he had met and first rescued his love. As the deep stream engulfed Magat, it grew into a mighty river.

Every year when the rains come, the Magat river rages. The townsfolk say that the hunter's spirit will not rest until he reaches the bones of his wife, buried in his yard at the edge of the town. If the water does not rise to that very spot, the Magat river will never be still.

Battle Island

The Legend of Apo Island

Apo Island is a small island in the Mindanao Sea near Negros Occidental province. It is a beautiful island surrounded by waters teeming with fish and other marine life. But it is also dangerous. Jagged rocks and swift, deadly ocean currents make it difficult for boats to land on Apo Island.

But once upon a time there was no island in this part of the Mindanao Sea. People there tell a strange story of how the island came to be.

On the southeastern tip of Negros Occidental there once was a rich village ruled by a brave chief named Apo Dauin. Apo Dauin and his people had come from the southern island of Mindanao. They had braved the waves and the open sea to settle here and build a new life

for themselves.

Apo Dauin's village was peaceful. There were plenty of beasts in the forest to hunt and plenty of fish in the sea to catch. The villagers were happy and content. And although the chief had guards to watch out for invaders, many of the villagers had set down their weapons for fishing nets or tools for farming. They did not expect enemies in their new home.

They were wrong.

One still night, when the moon was only half full, a small fleet of boats slid silently into the cove. The invaders were ruthless pirates! A guard called out a warning, but it was too late. The pirates were landing on the shore! Their boats were called *vintas,* and from the pattern on the sails it was easy to tell that they were from the southern island of Sulu.

The pirates descended on the village with bloodcurdling cries. Their sharp weapons glinted in the moonlight. The villagers scrambled for their weapons, but many were rusty from lack of use. Men and women fought bravely against the invaders, but no matter how hard they fought, they could not hope to win.

The battle lasted until dawn. Many of the villagers were wounded. They could no longer stop the pirates from looting their houses. The women tried to defend themselves with their kitchen knives. But they were tied up, gagged, and brought to the boats.

The villagers were angry, of course, and Apo Dauin was the angriest of all. "To the boats!" he shouted. "We must catch the pirates!"

But the villagers' fishing boats were no match for the swift and steady vintas of the pirates. Apo Dauin and his men pursued the vintas

to deep water, but it seemed that they had little hope of ever catching up with them.

Suddenly the vintas' sails loomed larger and larger. Were the villagers finally gaining on them? Then Apo Dauin's men realized what happened. The vicious pirates had turned their boats around. They wanted a sea battle!

Apo Dauin and his men were ready. Brown hands tightened their grip on their newly sharpened spears. The villagers waited for the onslaught. The enemy's swift vintas rammed the small fishing craft and the water churned white.

The villagers fought bravely. Many warriors were wounded in the battle. Some were thrown into the sea and drowned. It was a long hard fight, but in the end the curved blades of the pirates won over the hunting spears of the village warriors. The ocean turned red with blood.

The battle was over.

Apo Dauin and his brave men were dead.

Seeing this, the captured women in the vintas let out a loud wail. They prayed that they might join their loved ones in heaven rather than suffer at the hands of the pirates.

Their prayers were answered, because when the pirates put up their sails again, a huge storm arose. The vintas were tossed about like feathers in the angry waters. The pirates were good sailors, but no skill could battle nature's fury. The whole fleet sank.

The storm raged through the night. The next morning, the other villagers, those who had been wounded in the first battle, came out of their huts to see what was left of their village. A child saw it first. With

a loud cry he pointed to what seemed like a huge rock in the sea. It was near the spot where the second battle took place.

"It looks like Apo Dauin," said the child in wonder. "He came out of the water to guard our village!"

"Yes, that must be our Apo," said the child's grandmother, who had come out of their hut when she heard his cry. "It is Apo Dauin, risen from the sea to shield our village from further attacks."

Some of the people got into their bancas and paddled to the rock. As they came nearer, they thought they could see Apo Dauin himself sitting on top of the island. The wind seemed to carry the voices of their friends who had died in battle.

They tried to land on the new island, but the rocks and the currents made it impossible. "It is Apo Dauin making sure that no one will come in the dark to surprise us again," said the villagers.

Even today many mysterious accidents happen around Apo Island. Small boats are dragged down by the deadly currents. And some divers disappear, never to be seen again. It is said that the angry spirit of Apo Dauin is still there, watching over his beloved people.

The Queen Whom Love Forgot
The Legend of Mount Malindig

There once was a queen who lived in the island kingdom of Marinduque, in the southeastern tip of Luzon. Her beauty was famous, but few dared to know her. Her eyes were cold as diamonds set in steel, and her lips were frozen in a hard straight line.

Her name was Maria Malindig and she was a wicked ruler. When anyone displeased her she had him killed. All her subjects were terrified of her. Everyone said she was evil. Few realized that she was wicked simply because she had no one to love.

One day a storm rose over the sea. It raged for three days and three nights, but on the fourth day it stopped. The dawn rose clear and the sea was calm. When the people looked out onto the bay, they saw three huge ships with majestic white sails and many colored flags flapping in the wind.

In the palace Maria Malindig and her royal council watched the ships with great interest. Were they enemy ships? Or were they friendly ships seeking shelter from the storm?

They watched as a small boat was lowered from each of the three ships. The boats were rowed by several men. In the middle of each boat stood a man, dressed in robes so rich they reflected the sun and dazzled the eyes of all those watching.

The queen sent her chief minister down to the shore to meet the boats. The minister bowed to each of the three men and said: "We of Marinduque welcome you to our land. We would like to greet our visitors with a proper welcome, but it is difficult to do so without knowing who you are."

The eldest of the three men came forward and replied, "I am Laki, king of the eastern provinces of the Empire of Mu." He gestured graciously. "These are my companions. King Man-nga and King Pangikog." Both men bowed.

King Laki continued: "We followed the sun and crossed a hundred seas to find a kingdom ruled by a queen whose beauty is known far and wide. The storm drove us to your seas, but now we know that this is the kingdom we seek. We have come in the hope that one of us might win her hand in marriage."

The chief minister asked them to follow him. Together they made a long procession to the palace—the minister, the kings, and the kings' servants, bearing gifts for the beautiful but mysterious queen.

When the kings entered the palace they were struck dumb by the beauty of Maria Malindig. The queen herself quickly glanced at the visitors with a practiced eye. In a minute she had looked them over.

The first, King Laki, looked like an old gentleman. He had a loose lower lip that flapped when he talked. The second, King Man-nga, was good-looking but very short. The third and youngest king was Pangikog. He was tall and handsome, and the queen wanted to know him better.

When King Laki told her why they had come, Maria Malindig's cold heart let in a warm ray of hope. But she asked a lot of questions, for she was suspicious and did not trust easily. When her questions were answered, she said: "I know now that you are sincere, and I am honored. I have ruled my kingdom for many years. I welcome your gracious offer to share my burden...." Her voice became weaker, and for the first time in her life she was unsure. But she was a woman used to making choices, so she made up her mind quickly. "I choose Pangikog."

The kings sprang to their feet. "Your Majesty," King Laki said quickly, "It is our custom that a king marry only the woman he has won in a contest of skill. We cannot disobey the law."

"In my kingdom," said Maria Malindig icily, "my word is law."

Then King Pangikog spoke: "I am deeply honored, your Majesty, but I cannot go against the customs of my people. The matter must be decided with a contest, else I must return to my kingdom alone."

"Very well, then," said the queen. "We shall have a contest. The king that sails his ship the fastest wins my hand."

The day of the contest dawned bright and clear. People lined the beaches to watch the boat race. Maria Malindig and the royal household watched from the tower. All were eager to see the young and handsome

king win the race.

Soon the white sails could be seen. The people waited for the ships to come closer so that they could see who was ahead. Maria Malindig did not take her sharp eyes from the sea, and she knew before anyone else that King Laki was leading, followed by King Man-nga. King Pangikog's ship was last, far behind the other two.

Maria Malindig's heart sank in despair, but soon she became angry. How could Pangikog lose? Something as simple as sailing a ship...the man had to be a fool not to win the race!

She became angrier still when she thought of how she, the fairest of queens, did not deserve a husband as old as King Laki. She brooded, and the more she brooded, the more her eyes flashed with hate.

Quickly she left the tower. The ministers followed her to the temple of the gods. They were eager to see what she would do. Would she cast a spell to send a wind to King Pangikog and make him win?

But Maria Malindig had forgotten her spells in her anger. When she reached the temple, she screamed a high-pitched scream that was heard throughout the palace. "Worthless! You are worthless guardians of my fate! I long for warmth, but today you deny me that warmth! Why did you deny him victory? He should have been mine!"

And as her ministers watched in horror, Maria Malindig took a candlestick and struck down all the sacred idols. When the last one had fallen, the stones shuddered and the earth shook violently. A great wind rose from the sea. The sun turned black and darkness shrouded the kingdom. People ran, not knowing where to go, seeking safety from crumbling rocks and blowing winds.

In an hour the fury died down. The sun shone again and the skies were clear. The sea was calm. Everything was as it had been, except for Maria Malindig's palace. It had disappeared, and in its place a mountain had risen. The new mountain faced the bay, looking just like Maria Malindig had looked as she watched the race—proud and majestic.

The ships, too, were gone. In their place were three small islands. The people named the mountain after their queen with a heart of stone, and the islands after the three unfortunate kings who tried to win her love.

The Folly of the Seven Sisters

The Legend of Siete Pecadas

A long time ago, in the island of Panay in the Visayas, there lived a rich couple who had seven beautiful daughters. The girls had everything they desired. They had beautiful clothes and jewelry and all sorts of things to amuse them. They did not have to work. Their servants knew what they wanted even before they asked for it.

The girls became vain and selfish. They laughed at the customs of the people in their town. They only talked to others when they wanted to show off their new clothes and playthings.

Their father was upset with the way his daughters were growing up. He decided to take them to live for a while in a small house built on the bank of a wide river. He thought that fresh air and simple country life would change his daughters' habits. He forbade them to visit any

of the other houses by the river.

Although they complained, the girls seemed happy to play by the river. They seemed to enjoy swimming, boating, and fishing. What their father did not know was that they were also meeting with some young men from the other houses. These men were as rich and spoiled as they, and the daughters' bad habits grew worse.

"I am giving a party while my parents are away," said one of their boyfriends one day. "Why don't you come?"

The girls looked at each other. Their father would never allow them to go. It was Inez, the oldest, who answered, "We will have to be very careful. Nobody must hear us leave. We will climb the garden wall with the ladder the gardener uses to trim the branches. After supper, on Sunday." She turned to one of the boys. "Pick us up here, will you, Froilan?"

After supper on Sunday the girls met in Inez's room. They changed into their party clothes and, one by one, slipped out of the house through the backdoor. Carefully and quietly, they climbed over the garden wall.

No one noticed that the wind had a sharp edge to it, or that clouds were racing through the sky. The girls were not used to paying attention to anything but themselves.

When they got to the river, Froilan had a *banca* waiting. Not one of the seven sisters thought to look at the water. If they had, they would have seen that the waves were churning up the mud from the bottom, and that the boatman had a hard time steering the boat.

But Froilan's boatman knew the river well, and he brought them safely to the other side. "The water is high," the boatman warned Froilan

in a low voice. But Froilan ignored his warning.

When the seven pretty sisters arrived at the party, all eyes were on them. People whispered to each other, wondering aloud who they were and where they had come from. Singers serenaded them. Young men asked them to dance.

The girls' idle chatter soon filled the party. They enjoyed the attention. Not one of them thought about the time. They did not notice the wind blowing harder. It began to drizzle, but still they stayed at the party.

When the wind began to howl and the rain to fall harder, the sisters decided at last to go home. They ran to the river, where the banca was thrown about on the waves. "We must stay here," Froilan shouted, for by now the wind was roaring and the heavy rain stung their faces. "It is too dangerous to cross the river."

"But Papa will find out we're missing!" cried Inez. "No, we must leave now. Papa must not know. If you will not take us, let us use your boat. We will row home tonight."

So the seven sisters climbed into the boat, and Inez and Catalina grabbed the oars. But the wind was too strong. The storm was blowing in full force, and they could hardly see in all the rain. The boat pitched and rolled, and the girls could do nothing but hang on.

Suddenly Inez screamed. But it was too late! A split-second later, a big wave sent their boat flying into the air. The girls were hurled into the raging waters and swept out to sea. The bodies of the seven sisters were never found.

Time passed. The story was almost forgotten.

One morning many years later a fisherman discovered seven small islands out in the sea. He had never seen these islands before. Then he remembered the story of the seven sisters. He looked again. Each island was shaped like the face of each of the seven girls who had drowned in the storm.

The people of Iloilo still believe that the islands rose from the bodies of the seven sisters. Some nights you can hear strange sounds coming from the islands. Many say that it is the laughter and chatter of seven selfish and silly sisters who didn't know when to come in from the rain.

Sources of the Stories

"The Girl Who Fell from the Sky" is retold from "The Origin of Bohol Island and Its People," taken from *Philippine Folk Fiction and Tales* by Teresita Veloso Pil, published by New Day Publishers, 1997. (Pp. 53 - 54).

"The Greedy Neighbor" is retold from "The Legend of Lake Danum," taken from *Philippine Folk Literature: THE LEGENDS,* edited by Damiana L. Eugenio (Philippine Folk Literature Series, Vol. III), published by the National Research Council of the Philippines, 1985. (Pp. 173-175).

"Lord Laon and the Seven-Headed Dragon" is retold from "The Story of Kanlaon Volcano," taken from *Philippine Myths and Tales for Young Readers* by Maximo Ramos, published by Bookman, Inc., 1957. (Pp. 21-27).

"The Spring of Tears" is retold from "The Salt Springs of Salinas," taken from *Myths and Legends of Early Filipinos* by Felipe Landa Jocano, published by Alemar-Phoenix, 1971. (Pp. 62-65).

"The Hunter's Promise" is retold from "The Legend of the Magat River," taken from *Philippine Folk Literature: THE MYTHS,* edited by Damiana L. Eugenio, (Philippine Folk Literature Series, Vol. II). (Pp.155-156).

"Battle Island" is retold from "The Legend of Apo Island," taken from *Philippine Folk Literature: THE LEGENDS,* edited by Damiana L. Eugenio (Philippine Folk Literature Series, Vol. III). (Pp. 241-242).

"The Queen Whom Love Forgot" is retold from "The Fury of Maria Malindig," taken from *Philippine Folk Literature: THE MYTHS,* edited by Damiana L. Eugenio (Philippine Folk Literature Series, Vol. II). (Pp. 213-216).

"The Folly of the Seven Sisters" is retold from "The Legend of the Siete Pecadas," taken from *Stories and Legends from Filipino Folklore* by Ma. Delia Coronel, published by the University of Sto. Tomas Press, 1967. (Pp. 143-147).

For Further Reading

Coronel, Ma. Delia. *Stories and Legends from Filipino Folklore*. Manila: University of Sto. Tomas Press, 1967.

Eugenio, Damiana L. *Philippine Folk Literature: THE LEGENDS*. Philippine Folk Literature Series. Vol. III, mimeographed edition. Quezon City: National Research Council of the Philippines, 1985.

Eugenio, Damiana L. *Philippine Folk Literature: THE MYTHS*. Philippine Folk Literature Series. Vol. II, mimeographed edition. Quezon City: National Research Council of the Philippines, 1985.

Jocano, Felipe L. *Myths and Legends of the Early Filipinos*. Quezon City: Alemars-Phoenix, 1971.

Pil, Teresita V. *Philippine Folk Fiction and Tales*. Quezon City: New Day Publishers, 1977.

Ramos, Maximo. *Philippine Myths and Tales for Young Readers*. Quezon City: Bookman, Inc., 1957.

About the Author

Maria Elena Paterno is the author of several books for children, including *Volcanoes of the Philippines, Typhoon! All About Tropical Cyclones,* and *Earthquake!,* all published by Tahanan Books for Young Readers. She was awarded three Palanca prizes for Literature, including First Prize for Short Story for Children in 1991. She also received the Alfredo Navarro Salanga Award from the Philippine Board on Books for Young People.

Ms. Paterno received a master of education in reading from Harvard University. She is a graduate of the University of the Philippines, where she is currently a faculty member of the Department of English and Comparative Literature.

Ms. Paterno lives in Makati, Metro Manila.

About the Artist

Albert Gamos is a seasoned artist who has over a hundred publications to his name. A graduate of the University of the East School of Music and Arts, he ventured into film and advertising before he began to illustrate and design books for children.

Known for his rich and witty illustrations, he has won numerous awards, including an honorable mention at the 1985 Biennale Illustrations Bratislava competition for his picture book *The Love of Lam-ang,* and most recently runner-up at the 1992 Noma Concours for Picture Books Illustrations in Tokyo for his storybook *Pandaguan: The First Man Who Died.* In 1992 he was recognized by the Philippine Board on Books for Young People for his outstanding achievement in book design and illustration.

Mr. Gamos lives with his wife, Amelia R. Mendoza, and their five children in Angeles City, Pampanga.